Dove night songs

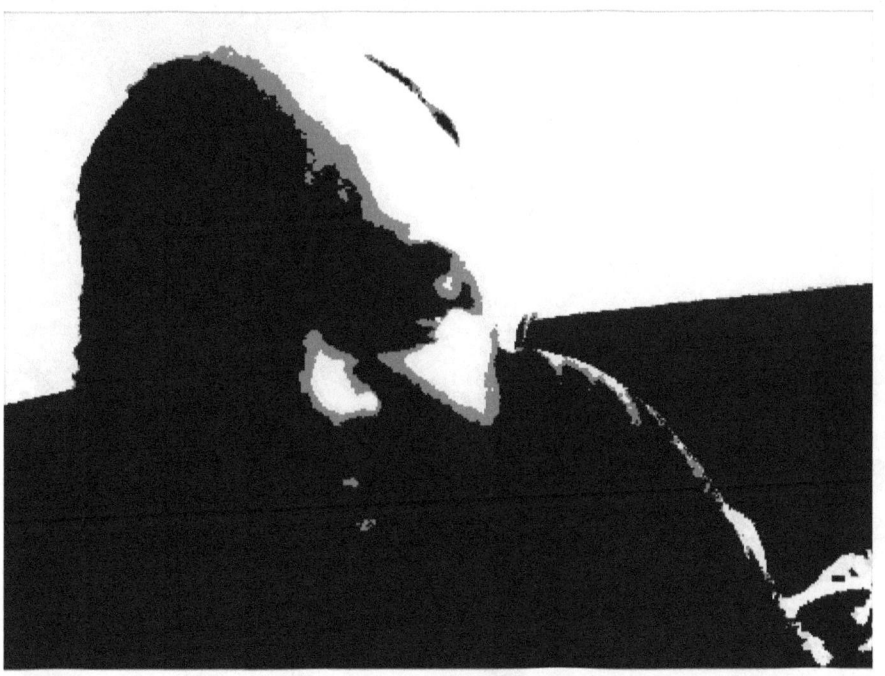

Dove night, the artist

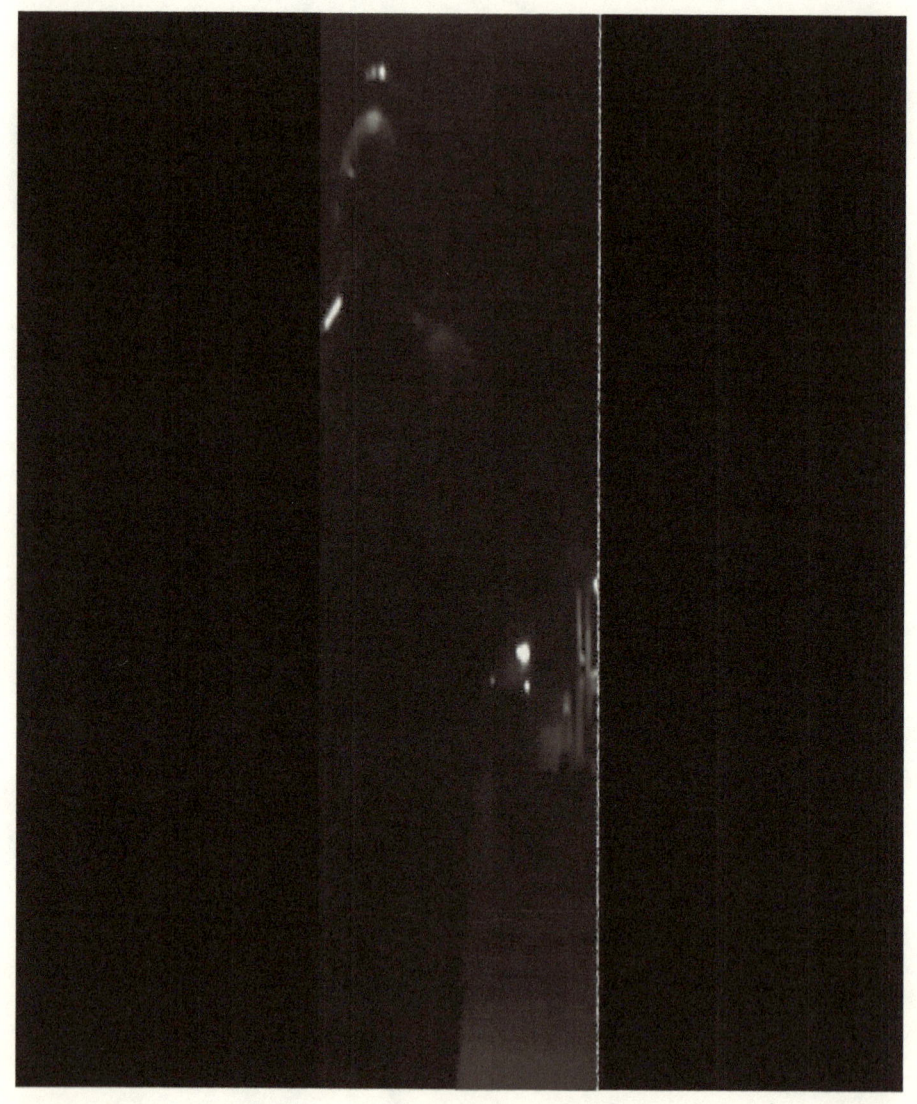

The singer, performer, songwriter, producer, arranger, musician has had a tough life, and I should know because he is me and that is the truth.

Let me talk about some songs on my catalog.

Trauma is a song written by me and David Waterbury about my early life and the tough times I had experienced when I first came to Los Angeles. I live on the streets, was robbed, destitute and I was in no good mood to write a love song at the time. I wrote it because I practically had to deal with chaos throughout my life, when I was first born into this world. I experienced trauma, through memories of abuse. The song was not released on sale at this time but was used to try to get a record deal with several indie and some major record labels but they turned me down. I was rejected, discarded, laugh at, and I felt my life was over but through resilience, a belief in god, I survived luckily.

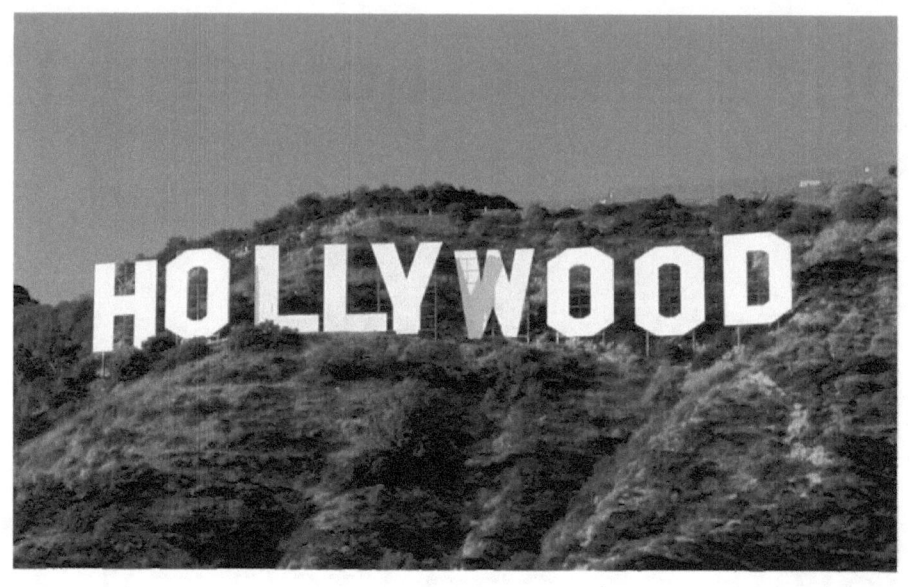

Hollywood, a place where I struggled to make my dreams come true

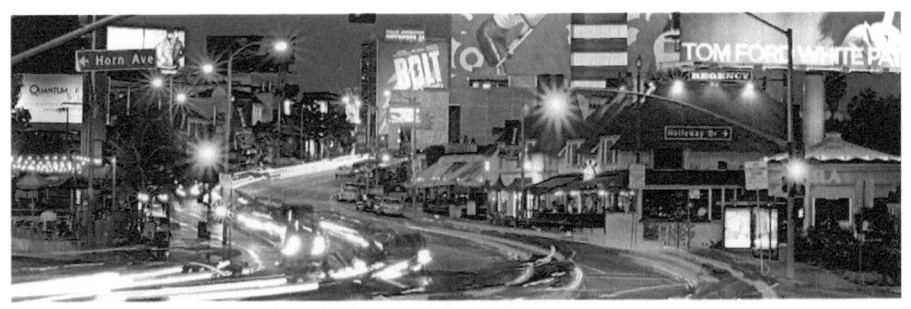

For an artist like me, the sunset strip, with the Roxy, the troubadour, the whisky a go go etc. was a place that was elusive for me in trying to make it to the top. I did sing over there at times but never was accepted.

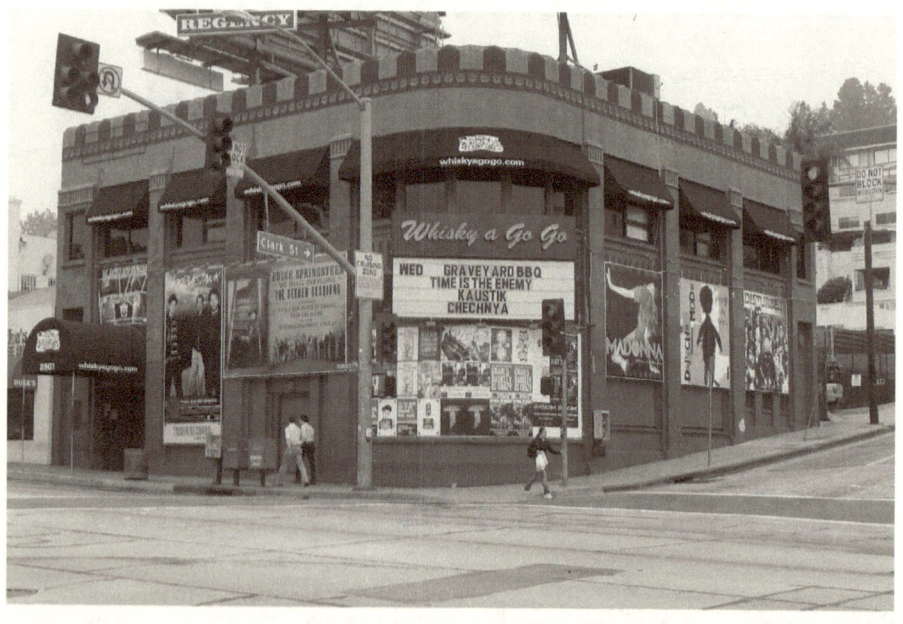

The whisky was elusive,

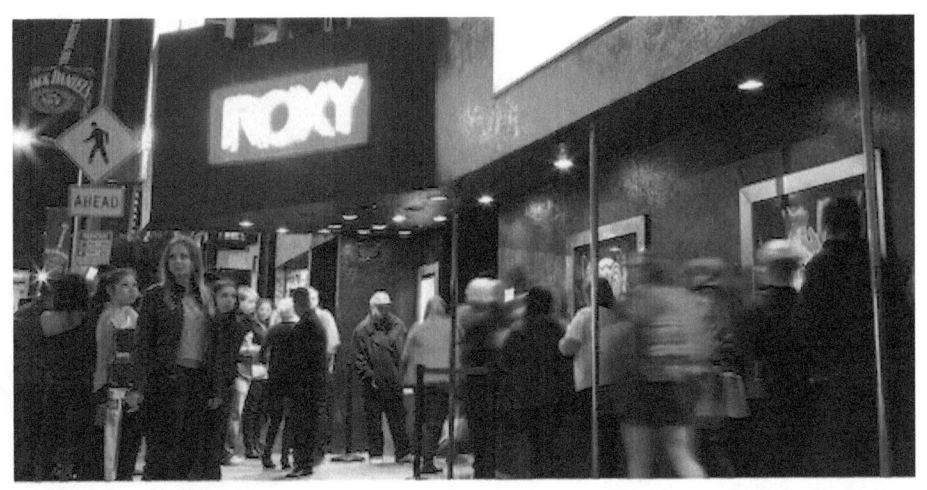

The Roxy was almost
impossible to get a gig
for a person like me
with a dream, to make
in the music business.

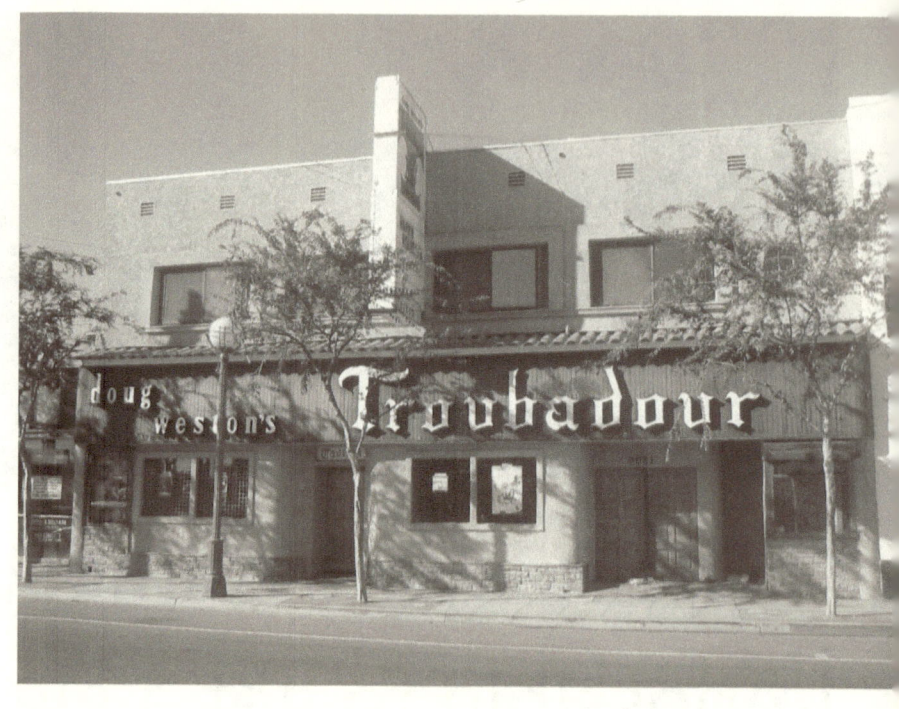

The troubadour was
impossible. I was told, I
had to be a big act to
play there, and my

dreams remain elusive,
as far as the sunset
strip is concerned.

I written a song called
"unique- a song
regarding some
incidents where I was
judged not to be a rock

star because of I was
seen as too fat, too big
and that was not fair to
me and other artists
who have talent as a
singer and /or a
songwriter or a
musician ,

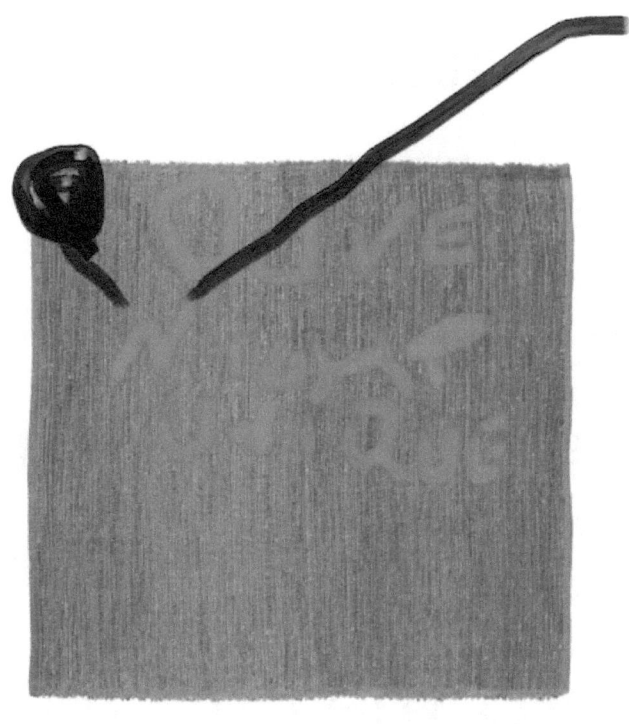

Unique cover on sale
at iTunes

I written a song called tragedy is not what I am , a rock ,country song about belief in myself ,that I can overcome obstacles, the song mention the true stories of dealing with failing exams

,classes in school, college and being subjected to a bad experience with a former friend who was on drugs. The truth is, is that being hooked on some drug can cause havoc and chaos for the

addict and his friends,
family.

The picture above is on sale at iTunes, and the title of the song is; tragedy is not what I am.

The unique video on vevo

Alternate titles for my unique song on iTunes is "landr 01, you can see it on Spotify

Alternate titles for my song "outcast "is Landr 18, you can see it on Spotify.

Alternate titles for my

song "forever on thru time is "landr 20", you can see it on Spotify. They were released on my cd, dove night, part 2the rock collection; it is on sale on iTunes.

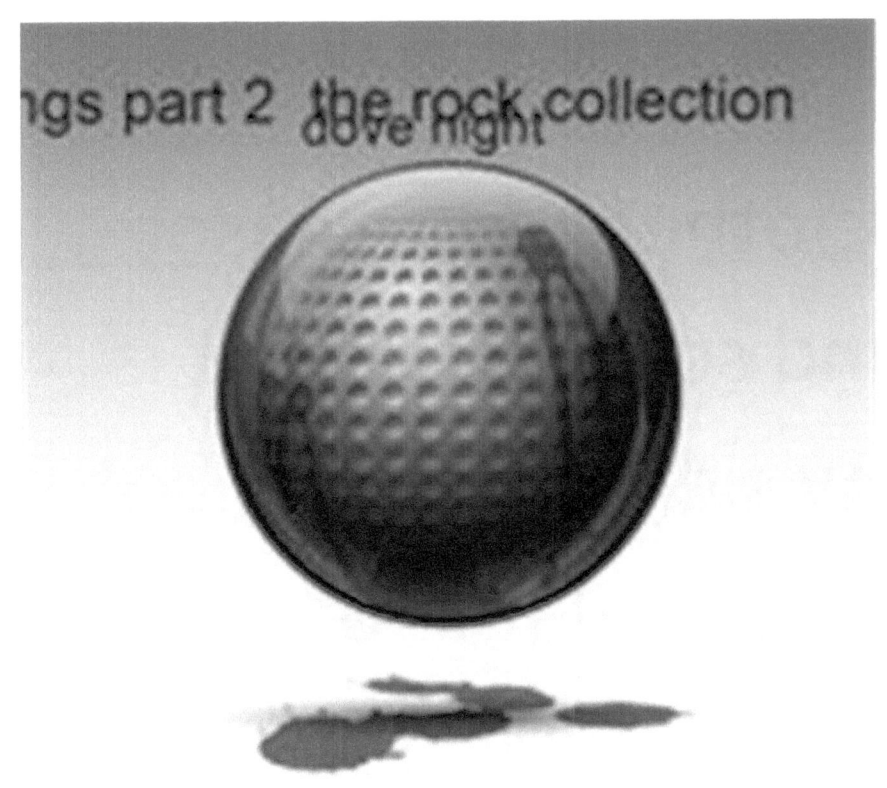

ngs part 2 the rock collection
dove night

This cd is on sale on
iTunes, I hope you
consider buying it

Another cd I released, and some will say it is my signature song but is say no! It's forever on thru time; it is on sale on iTunes. Below is the cd iTunes cover that is played on vevo.

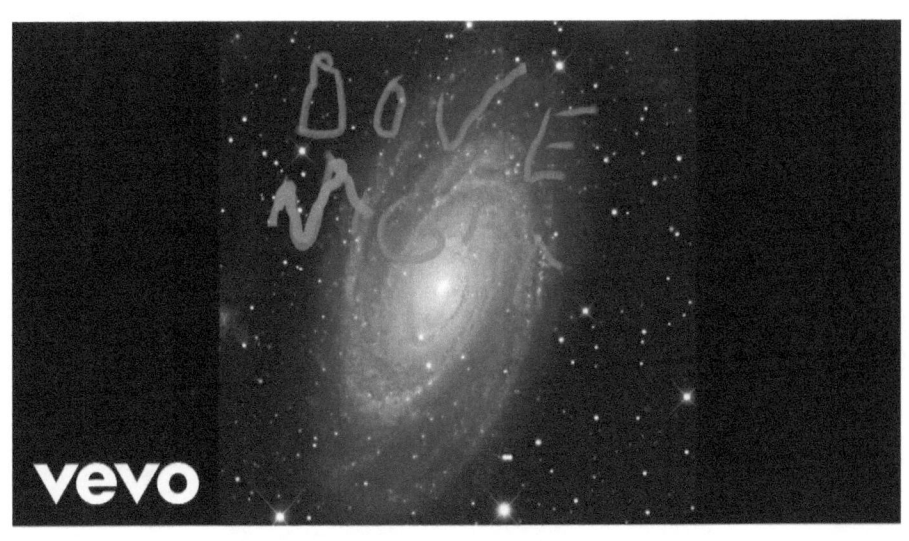

Forever on thru time is a song released in 2013, 2015 about falling for the right person after waiting for years. Here is the cd cover for both iTunes covers in 2013, 2015

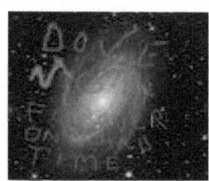

Released in 2015, on iTunes

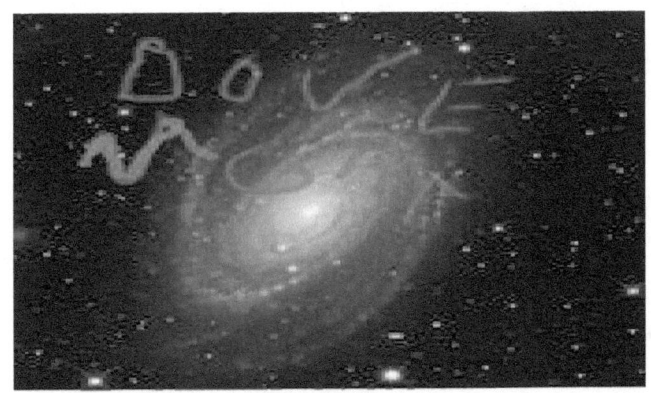

Cd, iTunes cover,
released in 2013.

Outcast is a song I co-written about feeling alienated from the world, the music industry, and a long time ago. It was about feeling alienated, as a child in high school and being subjected to criminal victimization, abuse.

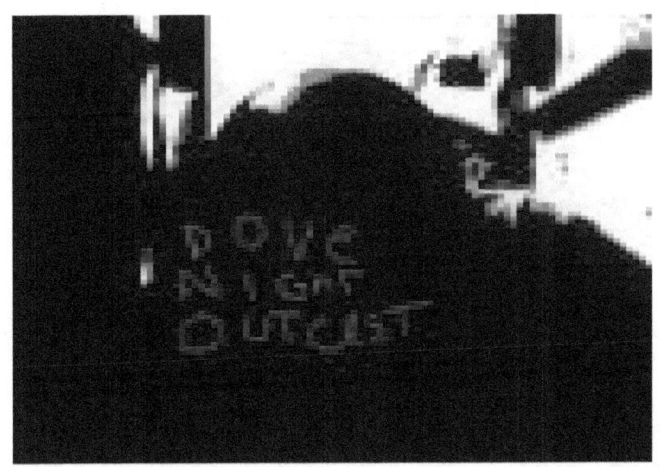

Cd, released on iTunes recently.

That is why I fell in love with you is a song written by dove night and Dave Waterbury. It is about meeting the right lover, and keeping them. The cd is on the

iTunes catalog if you
want to buy them.

t is why i fell in love with you

above night

You can buy all the songs on iTunes, google play, amazon, and many other stores, and you can see my videos on vevo, YouTube and many other sites as well.

Goodbye from dove night

www.ingramcontent.com/pod-product-compliance
Lightning Source LLC
Chambersburg PA
CBHW021853170526
45157CB00006B/2432